through darkness

r. anne

Dedicated to
all who find a home within these pages
because they did not feel safe in their own,
and to the love of my life, Emily.

introduction

This is my first book. I would be lying if I told you that it was not one of the hardest, yet most fulfilling, things I have ever done. Through Darkness is a collection of poetry and prose written over the last six years. Between the ages of 21 and 27, so much has changed. I finally explored my queerness, came out to my family, entered my first queer relationship which has now blossomed into a beautiful, somewhat unconventional, marriage. I have moved across the country and experienced the highest and lowest points of my mental illness. On top of all of that, I, like you, have been fortunate enough to have escaped a global pandemic with my life. Losing family and seeing friends lose loved ones only added to my urgency in producing this book. The past three years have been a very steep hill to climb; one that led to a cliffside that I've contemplated leaping from on many occasions.

From a very young age, an early sign of my OCD was that I felt constantly plagued by the idea that upon death, my art and writing will ultimately paint the picture of who I was. Social media is a façade that merely scratches the surface of who we are. You can either maintain that mystery in death or you can expand upon the surface layer you have allowed the world to see. That is the beautiful thing about the intersectionality of art and existence. Through art, we have the capability of existing infinitely. This is what I have chosen to do with Through Darkness.

My desire to achieve this infinite state of being has little to do with narcissism and everything to do with my longing for change. I hope for these pages to leave you in a different state than they have found you. My dream, more than riches or notoriety, is to foster change through these words.

I have asked myself several times, why am I writing this? Can it be that it is a sign of narcissism? Can it be that I think highly enough of my work that I have deemed it necessary to share it with the masses? Maybe. Or maybe, after more than two decades of depression, self-loathing, and suicidal ideation, I have finally deemed myself worthy enough of love and respect, resulting in the confidence to do this.

I say all of this not to validate my endeavors but to encourage you to do the same. That project you've been neglecting, that idea you've dreamt about but shied away from because the voices in your head have convinced you they weren't possible. They are.

If you have been looking for a sign, let this be it.
If you have been searching for a friend, let it be me.
If you are in need of a place to feel safe, let it be in these pages.
Let us go through darkness
together.

-r. anne

Self-Love

I would like to fall for myself

I want to trip on learned lessons
and land on new beginnings

Perspective

Every day
I begin to see this life through a new lens
from telephoto to wide angle
focusing more on our world
and less on my own

September

Few moments can compare
to the joy of a kiss
from the crisp fall air
gracing my lips

Art

A hand on my shoulder
a voice in my ear
whispers
"You and your burdens are welcome here"

Spring

After the rain
a flower still blooms
and after the pain
you surely can too

Paepcke

There is something immensely poetic about existing in the background of a memory. The sun is shining down on my left arm, my skin glowing and warm. A large and worn flannel separates the lush grass from my beige jumpsuit.

In this moment, I feel that the sky has never been quite as blue.

To my left, a family of six throws a football, delicate cheers following every catch.

To my right, a young man sits alone, laying down and gazing up at the clear blue sky. I can only imagine what thoughts he has chosen to pair with this serene moment.

Centered is me, a lonely little creature sitting with a tattered journal and pen in hand.

They will not remember me. But I will remember them.
Forever a ghost in the background, happy to observe from a distance.

Religion

My body
a temple
which none may enter
without bowing to the soul
who rules it

Self-Love (2)

My journey toward self-love
has no map to follow
but only one way to go

forward

Resilience

When the sun goes down
and the darkness ensues
the flowers do not falter
and neither should you

.

The Gardener

One cannot simply
wait
for success to come

you can wish for a garden
all day long
but it will not grow
until seeds are sown

Love, Mom

"The stars aligned so well when you were born, and
the world became immensely beautiful"

Content

To be alone and finally realize
you have all the company you'll ever need

Shattered

I sweep up the shards
of this broken heart
glue myself back together
and love the scars
you have left me with

Accompany Me

Let's build a ladder to the moon
and dance amongst stars
forget all of our fears
and live by our hearts

Reborn

Pain has changed me
in such beautiful ways

Now I find peace
in the way that it rains

Planetary

Carry me to the cosmos

I'll dance with dark matter
and wrestle red giants

Cry on the shoulder of Cassiopeia
play make-believe with Pluto

Whisper secrets to Jupiter
play dress up with Delphinus

I'll sing with the sun
and swim amongst the stars

that I know in my heart
I am destined to become

Before you try hard to hide those scars,
don't forget how far they have brought you.

5:25PM

I can't help thinking
that maybe

loneliness

is not my friend anymore

Home

The only home
I have ever known
is wrapped around my bones

Home (2)

The only home
I have ever known
filled with blood and bone
effort disregarded
only brokenhearted
a lonely garden
overgrown

Conundrums of Life

Tears
do not always indicate
sadness

As laughter
seldom indicates
peace of mind

Paranormal

Like a breeze you came along
& like a ghost
you were gone

The Race

How am I to outrun my fate
if the weight of my pain
holds me in place?

A Letter to You

I am sorry
sorry to the next
that will receive
this broken version of me

Bits and pieces
of the girl
I used to be

Without Ease

I cannot deny
the beautiful ways
that you have changed me
but I cannot lie and pretend
that a life without you
would not have been easier

I suppose life
was never meant
to be easy

Purgatory

Stuck between
the heavenly thought
and the hellish notion
that this is all
I will ever be

Resilient

I've wasted far too many nights
wondering what it was
in my ways of loving you
that chased you away

Those days are gone
lost like the love we shared
and today I am strong
resilient
in the face of heartbreak

Missing

Where has the poetry gone?
the craft of carefully stringing together
webster's finest
watching as thoughts metamorphose
into text on parchment

Where have the simpler times gone?
lost in a world of liquid crystal displays
and megabytes
slowly fading into an artificially lit world
the human experience turned
synthetic

Wishing Well

On this ledge I sit wondering
how many pennies must I sacrifice
to win a granted wish
if only I had known
falling into your depths
would be so easy
I would have kept my distance

Wilted

I am
a vase of dying flowers
in the center of an empty table
set for two

I have tried so hard to find peace
in all of the most painful places.

A Deadly Obsession

My wife brought home a skull fragment today. She found it while foraging for mushrooms in New Castle. "I knew you would go crazy for this!" she told me, as she carefully handed it to me. It seemed to be that of a deer. I took the piece graciously and began to analyze it. It was broken but I could easily make out the cranial sutures that wiggled across its surface. I ran my finger over them and couldn't help but think about the life that used to exist within it. My mind began to wander.

Why do I find myself thinking of death so often? I quickly realized that my thoughts regarding the fragility of life (or lack thereof) are rather constant. They were not exclusive to this gift, to this moment. But this did trigger something in me; I began to ask why. This question prompted another. Am I the only one who thinks this way? Am I the only one who thinks of our mortality numerous times a day? A brief sense of loneliness washed over me until I realized the answer to those two questions is a resounding no.

It was in no more than a few measly milliseconds that every social media account related to death that I have come across flashed through my brain like a flipbook. The conclusion came fast; I am, in fact, one of many people who ponder the realities of death quite frequently. Not only do we think of this, we blissfully bask in it. We romanticize it. We positively dwell upon it.

There are hundreds, if not thousands of stores dedicated to the selling of bones, wet specimens, postmortem photos, merchandise, and memorabilia, all in the category of death. Folks of every nationality, sexuality, class, and age visit these shops and quite literally rifle through death itself. We have found normalcy in this. We line our bookshelves with skulls for an "aesthetic." We watch true crime stories to put us to sleep.

Part of me thinks we are so detached from death, that we think of its dark and gruesome reality second to its mystery. Another part of me theorizes that we have grown comfortable with the idea of death due to the chaotic nature of our current political, social, and physical environment. It is as if the act of existing has become so mundane, that we have given up on its pursuance. Or could it be that existing has become so dangerous that we prepare for death before locking our doors behind us? Regardless, either of these truths result in a world in which many of us see death as little more than an ended heartbeat or a silenced breath.

Solitary

Who says it is a curse to die alone?

What is so wrong in dying with the only person
that has never betrayed me?

Recycle

What if instead of cutting yourself,
you use that blade to cut loose
all that has so desperately tried
to weigh you down?

Hush your cries of worry, dear,
not a single day is promised.

Cure

I often wonder
what you suffer from
hoping I can be the cure

Tranquility

My happy place
is within your arms
your "I love yous"
my favorite song

Blue-Eyed Boy

Never deny the perfect fit
of your lips between mine
or the words we exchanged
with a love so divine

Pastel

In this grayscale world
you are
an endless array of neon hues
a whirlwind of color
consuming time and space
a palette of wet paints
bleeding together
forming colors not yet named

You are
transcendent

Ablaze

Gazing up with wide eyes
your hand strokes my hair
while the other grips my throat

Mine tied by a neat double column
as I linger on your every hushed word

Labored breaths held in strained lungs
for fear I may soon combust
and collapse down to my knees
before you

You'd like that
wouldn't you?

You have been the catalyst for an
otherworldly transformation.

Closed Eyes

When the tears stopped flowing
paint-stained fingers
cover closed eyes

Minimal pressure
circular motions
darkness now studded
with neon stars

My pain becomes
my teacher

'

dear, I love you so
my heart shatters soft and slow
I beg you, let go

Longing

I long to kiss your every insecurity
to press my lips
against those hips
they have told you
are not small enough

I long to run my tongue down your spine
give you every reason
to spend each season
with your head on my chest
and my hand between your legs

I long to taste you
I'll use my tongue
for far too long
to trace every curve
and caress every tiny detail

I long to breathe you in
to lay beside you
to be inside you
to prefer reality to my dreams

Certain Tragedy

I loved
until you left me

I blinked
and you were gone

I sang
you covered your ears

From then on
you refused to hear

Intergalactic

The cliche tells us
the eyes are the windows to the soul

I must disagree

Your eyes take me
to new galaxies

Pollination

Maybe I am naïve.
I must be to find myself shocked that loving you would be accompanied by a pain I have never experienced.

I've learned that love and pain can coexist and, more often than not, they do. The cliché tells us that we would not know light without darkness. Without you, I have come to know a darkness unlike any other. I can only hope this is a precursor to knowing a new light.

"Don't waste energy thinking of me"

"I'd use every bit of my energy thinking of you and I often do with no regret."

I am your flower.
You are my bee.

Suddenly, pollination is much more than a science.

Merlot

Lost in a field
of red wine dreams come true
wishing to be found
by no one but you

Gravitational

Like waves by the moon,
I am moved
by you

BPM

You
have given a heartbeat
to the lifeless nights
I used to spend
alone

Supernova

And even after our love dies
like the stars in the sky
its light will shine on

Miraculous

It is quite miraculous that a six-inch thingamajig composed of metal, glass, and plastic is somehow spacious enough to hold entire lives.

Miraculous that, via this, you've painted a picture.

Miraculous that a collection of photos can become so much more, something far greater than the sum of its parts.

The picture you have painted is envied by many, reproduced by none. It tells a story large enough to fill a thousand pages.

It tells me that you are poetry. You are poems composed of metaphors my feeble mind cannot comprehend; Stanzas in languages I will never understand, an enigma, the mirage of a magnificent fountain in desolate land flowing with the purest water. As soon as my lips are graced by your sweet nectar, you vanish before my eyes.

Miraculous that you can exist in a world
you are too good for.
Miraculous that I am allowed
to exist in this world with you.
Miraculous that I can see you,
yet you are so out of reach.

Absolutely
miraculous.

Ache

Do not tell me you love me
make me feel it
love me so deeply
that those three measly words
will not suffice

Christine

On the mountainside, there is a striking demarcation
of where the 2018 Lake Christine fire burned nearly
13,000 acres.

It was started by a bullet.
Can you believe that?
Bullets take life in more ways
than we tend to think of.

From arid and ashen
to lush and green in an instant
the ground shows us
the moment the flames gave out.

Now, four years later,
we still see nothing
but the burnt remains of what once was
alongside the blooms of life
that survived and will continue to.

Science tells us that it can take up to 80 years for vegetation to regrow after wildfire has devastated the soil. That means that in my lifetime, I will more than likely never know the beauty that once adorned these mountainous views. While my soul cries for this devastation, I am reminded by my brown eyed girl that it is only a means for further creation.

This is because science also tells us that the natural pattern of life takes the land through an "ecological succession".

I prefer to call it a renaissance.

I may not see her lush greenery in my lifetime, but those who come after me will. For that, I am eternally grateful. Grateful that our world refuses to be overcome by the senseless flames that are forced upon her.

Let us learn from her. Never forget that even the wildest of flames cannot take down an unstoppable force.

Fiery

If it all ends in smoke and flames
I will never regret or be ashamed
of all of the ways I have loved you

Mercury

You
were as close to me
as the sun
and Mercury

Speechless

"Why do you love me?"
you said with a kiss
my voice falling silent
the words don't exist

Unspoken

You walked away and told me
this was goodbye
but the longing in your eyes
said otherwise

Explore

Don't you dare tell me
that I am your world
until you are willing to spend the rest of your days
exploring me

Explore (2)

Map me out
explore every curve
surf the waves between my legs
leave no stone
unturned

Explore (3)

Sink into me
and if you find sunken ships
or uncover shaking lips
promise me
you won't turn back

Maximum Security

I gave you my heart
in a little black box
with a master lock
and I swallowed the key

Buried

The memories of you
I cannot keep
so, I've boxed them up
and buried them
deep

Untangle Me

My body is in knots
only your hands can
untangle

Breathless

You have not taken my breath away
for I have given it to you
willingly

Gray Noise

Lay with me
let the background noise
be nothing more than
heartbeats
and heavy breathing

Luminous

You bring light
to the nights
I no longer spend crying

Passerby

I know that she broke you
but who would I be
to walk by shattered glass
and not pick up the pieces?

Solar Noon

Your soul is as bright
as the mid-day sky
stronger though still
for the dark
it denies

Unwise

I can feel you
throbbing in my hand
heart racing
hips trembling
self-control fading
wanting you is all I know
I no longer care to fight it

Waves crash into the shoreline
heavy breathing in moonlit darkness
wind rushing by tall beachgrass
whispered moans of loving being made
this is the soundtrack
to an ill-advised love

In the Beachgrass

Cold beach nights
sand in our hair
lightning strikes
in warm summer air
the fond memories
of our tame beginning

Regret

Some days
I wish I had never met you
most days
I remember the happiness
you've brought me
the lessons
you've taught me
it is then
I am reminded
that a world without you
is a world I have no business living in

Wishful Thinking

I wish I was her
to see through her eyes
to know your touch
better than I know my own reflection

Vivid

To wish myself rid of love for you
is to wish myself rid of colors true

Dreamer

These days
I look forward to going to sleep
for my dreams are the only place
in which I may love you
unapologetically
the only place
we can finally
be

Imprisoned amid

a longing for death

and a deep desire

to feel alive

Melodic

I wish I could explain
the way a soft melody
brings me straight
to thoughts of
you

Aromatic

That smell I adored so much
that musky aroma
now lingers on her sheets

Does she love that lovely aroma?
or does she carelessly clean the sheets?

Returning them to their cotton breeze scent
knowing damn well
I'd neglect them for far too long
just to feel you near

Atlantic

I will never forget his lips

Soft as a summer breeze
caressing a sunburnt smile
sweet as the cake we shared
with stomachs far too full
filled with words eloquent and kind
willing to meet mine without
any hesitation

Deluge

No matter how blue the sky is
life seems to find a way
to flood us in darkness

What matters most
is how we escape

Transferal

Despite the pain I feel within
I'd gladly endure yours again and
again

Lightning

Our love was
bright and sudden
brilliant and terrifying
I have come to learn
that the greatest things in life
usually are

May the sound of your snores forever be my lullaby
and may your bitter morning kiss
forever be my wakeup call.

M

I remember standing there with you
under the trunk
of the fallen tree
in the golden sun
with the biggest smiles
we had ever had

Prisoner

Constantly dragging
a ball and chain
around a broken ankle

A compound fracture
gone necrotic

Yet I press onward
carrying the weight
of suicidal ideation
and the inability
to follow through

Often unsure if my words
~~will~~
should
be heard or silenced.

"Normal"

For a moment I felt
normal
I looked out the window
saw the man in the Nissan Xterra
let his blaring music fill my ears
and though the moment was brief
everything felt
okay

Tease

Let the thoughts of me
dance circles around your mind
in black and lacy lingerie

The Journey

Nihilism is a long road
often unpaved
embellished with bright green patches
microbiomes teaming with life
where the purple asters play
and the bumblebees take refuge

Though this road is long
she gently nudges time along
to move by effortlessly

Don't stop until you reach the aspen trees
and where the road T's
where left is right and right seems wrong
which way will you turn

Service cuts out here
no maps and no one to call
to aid you in this decision

Choose carefully
as she can lead you to
endless imagination and fearless flight
or to your absolute
detriment

Sink or Swim

I feel like I've gone mad

"If you can swim,"
he said,

"Allow yourself to fall into madness
without the fear of sinking"

With how rare true love seems to be
why won't you accept mine?

The Intangible Medium

I would fill a museum
with the contents of my heart
if only true love
were a form of art

Envisage

These days
when I look into the mirror
I see a masterpiece

Painted by the universe
unveiled by you

Resilient

Before declaring yourself weak
be sure that your idea of strength
is within the realm of possibility
and within your realm of inner peace

Time

She resembled an hourglass
not only in her figure
but in her ability
to never let time control her

She was terrifyingly
infinite

Finality

I beg you dear
do not leave me here
without a whisper in ear
of those three final words

Escape

The strings I attach
tend to be nooses
pulled taut
by a hasty escape

Kaleidoscope

Do not classify me
as a case of pure craziness
for living life
through the lens
of endless imagination

Film

When I begged you to take a photo with me
I told you it was just for fun
but truth be told
I knew it was the only way
I could be with you in
permanence

Take me unto you
your temple of a body
never let me go

Neglect

Planted in rotting soil
within a broken pot
doused in acid rain
never given a chance to
truly bloom

Wonder

Instead of picking that daisy
plucking her love-me's
and love-me-not's
I decided to leave her
because no one
should ever have to wonder

Furtherance

Sacrifice
is necessary for furtherance

After all
the sun does burn
to light our way

It was not long before our sweet, sweet love
became a bitter lust.

Fantasy

We pay for
romance films
and love stories
because happy endings
seem like a far-fetched fantasy

Ephemeral

You are the shore
I am the waves
crashing against you
despite the pain

Irresistible

The curve of her hips
the pink of her lips
beckoned me in
I could not resist

Self-loathing killed the creative.

The End of a Story

As our story went on
and I dog-eared bad days
that right hand corner
became too thick
to carry

Endless Gratitude

It is with a heart filled with gratitude that I thank you for reading my first publication. Writing a book is something many of us dream of and I feel so fortunate to have done so at the young age of 27.

Once upon a time, I did not believe I would make it past 17 years old. I believed this world was too harsh for me. I believed I existed as something less than human, unworthy of life, let alone being heard. You hold in your hands proof that I made the right choice in staying.

I hope that you have found a home in these words or a friend in this soul of mine. I hope I have shown you that while pain is unavoidable, it can birth art in an infinite number of forms.

We exist on purpose.

I am so glad you've allowed my words a comfy space within your existence.

Until next time,
r. anne

ISBN: 979-8-218-13684-0